# War Story

**Vietnam War Poems
By Gerald McCarthy**

 The Crossing Press, Trumansburg, New York, 14886

Acknowledgments

Some of these poems first appeared in

Magazines: *New American & Canadian Poetry, Aisling, Bitteroot, Wisconsin Review, The Stone, Bartelby's Review, Alleghany Poetry, Jam Today, Northeast, Spring Rain, Ragged Oaks, The Experimentalist.*

Anthologies: *Demilitarized Zones, Veterans after Vietnam,* East River Anthology, Perkasie, Pa. 1976

Drawing by Raymond Larrett
Cover Graphics by Karl Wolff

The Crossing Press Series of New Poets

This project is supported by a grant from The National Endowment for the Arts in Washington, D.C. a Federal agency.

Library of Congress Cataloging in Publication Data
McCarthy, Gerald, 1947-
    War story.

    (The Crossing Press series of new poets)
    SUMMARY: Poems depicting life on the battlefield, the return to the United States, and adjustment to civilian life.
    1. Vietnamese Conflict, 1961-1975--Poetry.
[1.  Vietnamese Conflict, 1961-1975--Poetry.
2.  American poetry]  I.  Title.
PS3563.A25917W3        811'.5'4        77-23320
ISBN  0-912278-87-0
ISBN  0-912278-86-2 pbk.

for *Turner*

*Black riders came from the sea.*
*There was clang and clang of spear and shield,*
*And clash and clash of hoof and heel,*
*Wild shouts and the wave of hair...*
                                    *Stephen Crane*
                                    *The Black Riders*


*In the fall the war was always there,*
*but we did not go to it anymore.*
                                    *Ernest Hemingway*
                                    *In Another Country*

I

## WAR STORY

1      Med Building

They brought the dead
in helicopters and trucks
and tried to piece the bodies back together,
shoved them in plastic bags
to be sent home.
Sometimes there was an arm or leg
leftover,
it lay around until the next shipment;
they made it fit in somewhere.

2       Plowed fields,
        the eyes
        stare at the barbed wire
        and the MP armbands.

3      Two soldiers
sit under the glare of an electric light
in a deserted tent
that stinks of men
just passing through.

4      My clothes dripping wet,
I crawl into my cot
under the safety of the mosquito netting,
fall asleep,
the sound of rain against the canvas.

5    Sunny morning
     seven Vietnamese kids
     steal C rations
     near tin shacks
     where marines screw their sisters
     at night.

6  First month

It was the beginning of summer,
year of the monkey,
everybody I knew well wore khaki.

Boyd got dysentery and lost twenty pounds.
It was the start of the monsoon,
I got transferred
and Doug went stateside.

No one ever shot anybody,
but we used to read about it
in the papers from home,
or miss a friend in the chowline some morning.

7    Flares in a night sky
     lighting up the place
     like a football field.
     Ammo belts
     strung over shoulders,
     I remember the time
     I was a newsboy
     with the sunday morning papers,
     throwing the headlines.

8    We found him
     his chest torn open,
     shirt sticky brown.
     A corporal with a bayonet
     cut off his ears,
     and kicked the body
     in passing.

9   They shot the woman in the arm,
    four of them
    raped her
    and killed an old man
    who tried to interfere;
    and later killed the woman too.
    She was the enemy.

10    Wading through streams
       rifles overhead,
       they photograph us for *LOOK*
       and some idiot smiles.

11    Hot sun,
      I walk into a whorehouse
      pay the girl
      unbuckle my pants
      and screw her
      sweat sticking to my fatigues
      small legs grasping my back
      her slanted eyes look up at me
      as I come.
      Outside the tin-roofed hut
      another GI waits his turn.

12    That night in the bunker,
      we shared some smoke
      and stared out at the stars.
      Then,
      the mortars blasted
      choking sulfur
      shoving the magazines in
      round after round
      deaf,
      blinded,
      hugging the dirt,
      I pissed my pants.
      Later,
      confusion gone,
      you all shot to shit,
      you black bastard.
      Fuck.

13     War Story

The machine-gun fire has us pinned down
in the trees.
Down the line
somebody's hit bad
screaming for the corpsman.

We wait for the word
to move out
and nobody changes the reel,
we don't get time for intermission.

Everyone's up
moving across the rice paddy,
the lieutenant gets his face blown off.

We make the ridge
and there's nothing there,
except a hundred and fifty naked women,
all ex-playboy club bunnies
all nymphomaniacs,
who say to us in one voice:
"Ford has a better idea."

14    In the early morning the working party came and filled in the remains of the bunker with sand. The bodies had been removed the night before, but the stench lingered. Soon the earth was worn down smooth by the boots of the soldiers. They moved off to build another bunker along the line.

Clinging to a bush was a dirty piece of utility jacket. A breeze was blowing in off the ocean. It rattled the pop cans on the concertina wire and made hollow, tinny noises.

## 15    Sniper

I lay down in the sand
the jungle noise settles around me.
Pete lies dead a few yards in front
toes dug into the ground.
Sweat runs down across my chest
and I shiver
searching the trees.
A long silence surrounds the noise,
I wait for movement.

The sound of a limb breaking
and I open fire towards it,
but he's got me.
Goddamn.
Knocked backward, rolling to one side
it happens all at once.
He's got me.
The arrow sticks in my chest
and in the distance I can hear the bugles,
the pounding hooves.

Light blinds me,
I lie hands and feet tied
feeling the heat.
Jesus Christ, somebody pull the switch.
I'm sorry.
A beetle crawls along my arm
bites me near the elbow.
I can't move.

16      Going home
        khakis creased with dirt
        I stand in the bus station,
        hoping someone
        will notice the ribbons
        pinned above the pocket
        of my shirt.

17      Well, I said, I came back.
        Grandpa pulled the hat down over his eyes
        smiled at me in his sleep.
        They asked if I wanted breakfast,
        some coffee maybe?
        Had it been a long ride?
        My father looked older.
        I smoked a cigarette,
        watched the shadows leave the backyard
        back into the old house,
        my stepmother's chatter,
        the old man's sadness
        so early in the morning.

18      Up in Cortland,
        they erected a plaque
        to the memory of private Jim Galutz,
        who shot 210
        on the rifle range
        in boot camp,
        when the war was a second-hand whisper
        after the lights went out.

19    John Bradt said, It'll be all right
      when he gets home.

      The farmers in Hale valley are waiting
      for the sun to rise.
      The train winds slowly
      through the mountains.
      A voice of strangers
      knocking politely
      on doors.
      The soldiers are coming home,
      they carry the sadness with them
      like others carry groceries
      or clothes in from the line.
      There is no music in the parade;
      the sound of their coming
      waits at the bottoms of rivers,
      stones rubbing against each other
      in the current.

20    The rain beads on the screen door
      and taps out drumbeats
      on garbage can lids.
      I stand outside
      getting wet in the dark.
      I've come back again;
      the rain moves slowly through the leaves
      passes down in the stones
      making puddles.
      I rest myself against the rain.

21    Watching the silent parade
on Main Street,
the American flags lined up
on parking meters,
I feel strange.

The American Legion passes by
they're all going to lunch today
together;
guest speaker: the mayor—a veteran of WW II.

I go into a clothing store
to buy some socks.
The manager brushes past me
as I leave,
donning his VFW hat.

In front of the war memorial monument
the police stop cars,
the veterans shoot their rifles.

I cringe a little
and hurry past some old ladies
waiting for their veteran husbands.

The bank is closed.
The movie marquee says: John Wayne in...
I realize
I am a communist.

22    Voyeur

The women rise from the water
wading through the surf,
shaking the water from their hair,
caught in the moonlight,
bodies thousands of wet drops.

I can hear them laughing
above the roar of ocean;
talking to one another
lying down on the beach.

They stretch themselves
warm breeze a blanket
beneath the stars.

II

## ARRIVAL

There it is again
the roll of cars in wet streets
hours crushed together in the rain.

I come back to the voices
to their eyes
to a hand turning up a collar in the crowds
to a dark street in the snow.

I lower myself back
my feet in doorways
silence like a rope behind me.

Yes, this must be the right street
and they must be my friends
the stares buttoned to their lapels.
I follow them all the way.

This is where I wanted to get off
in a new winter
on this avenue of trees
the sound of wings
and the wind
wrapping itself around me.

The same glow in windows
and my hands on the hours
on the empty glasses.
The days stuffed in my pocket
like old addresses
and my coat too thin
for this cold.

## RIDING WEST FROM CLEVELAND, OHIO

Riding west from Cleveland, Ohio
the smell of fields and cold air
fireflies blinking in the chill.
Football heroes haunt the small towns,
girls bare themselves on back seats
while their mothers turn restless in sleep
and the lights are going out.
Fall begins its movement
crickets rub their legs together
in the dark,
a nighthawk circles toward home.

## JOYRIDE

I have been watching
the way the land rolls
up from the lake,
how the road looks
from the air.

This is the last flight.
The pilot lets me take control:
the lines of farms
a gradual rise
out of the valley.

Now ease off on that stick,
we are away from it.
The hills ahead
filled with trees.
The blue sky ahead
open
clear.

## GOODNIGHT JONNIE LOGAN

The streetlights
are yellow circles
in the snow.
The baseball field
frozen
wood bleachers all ice.

John Loganski played baseball
for the Milwaukee Braves
changing his name to Jonnie Logan.

The little league diamond
on the north side of town
is dedicated to him.
The wooden sign says: Logan Field.

Standing here,
the night with voices of desperate men,
running away with winter
falling around them;
I am home again.
The streets like old friends
shaking hands
and turning away.

## A LAST LETTER TO ELIZABETH

Goodnight.
The way we move outward
is a sign
the motion will continue.

The streets are deserted
it hasn't snowed since you left.
Time stretches its face thin,
I feel it slipping around me.

The days go on,
the night waits.
It's all right.

The last letter I got from Aubrey,
he said: "That hippie pussy is ok,
but it don't beat a chick with a little soul."

He was dead three weeks later,
on Operation Union 2
near Chu Lai, South Vietnam.

This is the place we have come to,
the air heavy with rain.

## JANUARY 1971

I wake up screaming.
It has been a winter of thieves.
I can hear their voices
in the dark, they are coming for me.

I look for the outline of her breasts
beneath the covers,
the hours have all run together,
and I am afraid.

My back pressed against this night
I can see the glow of cigarettes,
I can hear the coarse laughter.

This is the way it's always been,
I speak their language
and could never give up
without a fight.

## POEM

It's March.
Winter walks away from us.

I grow inward
like a vine
spreading its fingers.

I feel the rain on my face
the quickness in my limbs,
I come out from the blindness
my body becomes my own again.

In the woods
the streams are starting to break free,
the sounds of water moving over rock
echo in the trees.

I see the lake below
the weak spots in the ice,
I rise from the cold
a new silence in my voice.

## AMBUSCADE

In the distance
the deer watch us.
We cross a field
and follow their tracks
in the woods.
The sound of water
falling over sheets of limestone
calls us from silences.
Dark filters through the trees,
there is no way home.

# III

## CONNECTIONS

Time etches its blueprint against my eyes.
She was telling me she had a vision,
I told her about that day in Harrisburg
when the car broke down.
She laughed across the miles
of telephone connections.
I thought about Barbara
weekends in Rochester, New York,
taking the long bus ride back
the years have made us both strangers.
Annie is dead,
killed in a car accident.
I want to lose myself in the mountains.
My eyes are tired.
She says:  I have to go now.
I try to smile at her through the phone,
try to tell her that it's not all right.
I reach for the change
and notice my fingernails are dirty.

## EPISODES

The rain leaves the afternoon, grey light lasts
too long in the trees. I watch the dogs chasing
an animal in the dusk, their breaths fogging.
Night stretches over the shadows. I am walking
along a road and can hear the distant noise of
water. Two people pass by. One is a man in a
raincoat and dark glasses, the other is dressed
like a ship's captain.

I'm sitting in a park across the street from
a Kirby's Shoe Store, somewhere in New England.
A thin guy in janitor clothes has passed out on
the lawn in front of me. It's one of those days
nobody remembers. The evening is full of cars.

Quite recently in South America, a man was dis-
covered with two noses, with an unknown green
plant that grew from one set of nostrils. The
man is a deaf mute and very old. He does not
respond to sign language. Currently, doctors
have him in a private suite in a hospital in
Buenos Aires. Many efforts have been made to
communicate with him. As yet, all have failed.

## WHAT THE DREAM WAS LIKE

*for Joe & Fran*


They came with anger in their throats
beers in their hands
IBM computers in their eyes.

The cards drop from the machine
in rows of orderly sound.
My old man pushes the right buttons
flashes his life in front of the color t.v.
nodding into a seven p.m. doze
feeling the tapes going around
like twin yellow suns
inside his brain.
The clicking noise wakes him,
the tiredness fits him close.

In the morning
he begins each day's
long walk to death.

Cards shuffling
in the machine,
separated
divided
pushed together in piles
stacked in metal bins.

## APERTURES

In the middle of a yawn
the curtain opens
& a pair of woman's breasts
thrust out
like piers along the shore
that catch the force of storms.

The lady says she's glad
I came back.
My mouth is full of candybar
& everything I say sounds like:
oogah-oogah.
I smile through chocolate teeth.

Yesterday it was cold
& it rained all afternoon.

At the turn of the century
Thomas Alva Edison invented light
& his dog curled up beside the fire
with a bone.

## I'LL BRING YOU A FROZEN CHOCOLATE PIE

OK, I surrender.
I'm twenty seven & feel funny
buying a tube of Clearasil
at the corner drug store.

Sometimes I sneak a few comic books
or the latest copy of Skin magazine.
I drink cokes forever.

My friends are getting serious
they tilt their faces towards me
asking: "Well, what are you gonna do?"

In the dark booth
the priest said: How many times?
Oh, it was good afterwards
walking into the daylight.

In alleyways I wait
for young high school chicks
who've taken a wrong turn somewhere.

I get so hungry
I eat the fingers on my hand.

When the screaming stopped
I was lost in morning,
there were a line of boats
slipping beneath the water.

When the screaming stopped
she was lying there
& I could not wake myself.

## THE WATCHERS

Because she was jealous
the spirit of the wood
turned the princess into a vine.

The frogs saw her
& their drunken language
echoed off the pool.

Nek-ked! They cried to Harry
wheeling past the edge
one autumn afternoon.

He stopped & lit a cigarette
& wondered who had spoken.

Harry the Hat sat back
& thought, looking around
into the woods.

Suddenly he felt
a hand on his shoulder.
It was the princess
awoke from her long sleep
as a vine.

Harry stared & saw that
she was indeed naked
& very pretty
& smiling.

Harry took off his hat
& hung it from the handlebars.
Then he took her hand
& walked into the woods.

# MERMAID

I follow you down
the winding stairs;
no, it's just a staircase
with two landings.

On the first
you touch my arm and look back,
your neck tilted up, swan-like.

We descend, hand in hand
and at the door
you pull me towards you,
and of course I smell the ocean
in your hair.

And it'll be like that forever -
the goodnight kiss at the door,
the small voice going on and off,
on and off.

If I were a watchman
in a lighthouse,
I would let you lead me
beneath the waves,
down to where you sleep
in the dark green sea grass.

## SONG

The birds return to their nests
in the walls.
It's the end of March
and the wind has been here for days.
I come to myself in the late morning
walking in the trees.
It's a mistake I've made before.
There's nothing but shadows in these woods
and a man walking up ahead.
The dark morning follows itself
into afternoon,
it begins to rain.

## FREE FALL

I have the right to jump if I want to,
to open the door of the plane
and leap into the wild blue yonder.

She was telling me
about her mother,
I was looking at the blond hair.

She helped me into the parachute
and tightened the straps.
I tried to grab her breasts,
I suppose it was something
about her face.

The door opening
wind knocking me down
then pulling me through.

Looking back
her hair streaming
cold air making her blush.

And then the night
reaching up like a wave
pulling me under.

## CASTELO DES MOUROS: Sintra, Portugal

I stand in the ruins
of a garrison built by Moors.
It is November,
the morning wind against the stone.
In the distance
the ocean to Africa.

My first memory was death
dressed as a woman,
the sun behind her body
rising,
mother gone these years
among the stones.

Beneath my feet
the path is covered with moss,
wind trapped in the rock;
the storm in the trees below
a woman shaking her hair free.

I go on walking in this outpost,
centuries fallen to the dust of walls.
Silence eats out its heart
beside me,
language itself grown old.

# LETTER TO MY FATHER

*And in Iowa I know by now*
*the children must be crying*
*in the land where they let*
*the children cry...*
*—Jack Kerouac, On the Road*

There are places that we come to
without knowing;
as if waking from a long ride,
stepping off onto a deserted platform
the sign swinging out above our heads.

The train passing
no faces in the windows,
nothing but rain
and lights fading in the distance.

The wind,
the voice of a woman
singing,
the cries of birds
in a morning.
The days hung on wire.

We grow separate,
old men in streets
who think of nothing but themselves.

# IV

## FINDING THE WAY BACK

Morning.
Two sparrows sit on the tin roof
puffing themselves up
like old men in a park.
The longest war of this century
refuses to be ended.
I watch them signing their peace
with twelve different pens
live on t.v.

I remember the ocean
the breeze off the water
sunlight through the curtains of rain.
The young men running
darkness falling around their shoulders.
The children gone
their hearts in open throats.
The faces
the last columns of smoke
tearing the pages from my eyes.

There was never anything to come back to.
Aubrey knew it at Binh San
under the afternoon sun
staring into death.
My brother
I went on living.
There was nothing else
I could do.

## THE WISH

A morning in childhood
when he woke early
and could smell the wind
in the leaves.
The sunlight caught
in wet grass
and all the women going away,
his father
walking with him,
saying his mother was dead.

*

A woman
on a bridge in fog,
leading him from the stream
her body in the grass,
the taste of rain
on her mouth.

*

A dark street,
the faces pressed in windows.
A deserted station
in the snow.
A hospital room
and a nurse with heavy thighs
and white stockings.
An ache in the fingers
for surfaces.

*

The motion,
the open-ended days,
long rides to the ends of highways.
The angry way the other cars
went by at dusk,
their running lights on.
The roads built
to reach each other.

## TRIPS
*[for Peter Revson]*

*To know the universe itself as a road,*
*as many roads, as roads for traveling souls.*
*—Walt Whitman, Song of the Open Road*

The wall, the hot ash of recognition,
one hundred and fifty miles an hour
and the wheels locked on.

The tight roar exploding into white light,
and the hands dropping away,
fire eating up the asphalt.

A South African sun burning,
and the afternoon clear and bright,
washing over the dull screams.

\*

A phosphoresence, a shell inside a shell,
waking the first time:
a room in morning, the ocean spread out
beneath his window, a dark haired woman
walking towards him across the sand.

Costa del Luz. Cadiz. Portimao.
The names seemed more important
than anything.

He brought his hands to the side
just at the moment he felt it go
felt the whole thing slide right.

*

The opening, the other side,
another morning further back.
Going the distance along the path
miles in between full of sleep.
And the woman said:
It's a dragonfly, it'll sew up yr lips.

Forever. The tunnel.
The motion. The idea of God.

The boy hid a fox
inside his coat
and it ate the boy's heart.

All the ways out are the same.
That falling. The rush of air against the metal.
The boy is not asleep.
He is waking.

*

Memory, a face in the rain,
a fine mist on the water.

The voice calling
again and again.
The flights. The repetition.

The sound getting louder.
A street, a steady ringing of bells.
The sea, the waves in night storm
each crest, each breaking,
lifting him up.

The feel of wind, the light returning
one more time.
The wall. The hot ash of recognition.

## THROWING OUT THE MUSE

1   August, another summer pulls the sleep away.
    I was walking through yellow flowers.
    She said: Their name is absence.
    A trout jumped on the pond, a white butterfly
    settled in the chicory weeds.

    A heron rises from the berm near the water,
    and becomes the distance.
    If I could remember only the edge of cliffs,
    rain dancing on the rock.

    I make myself sick.

    Last night town punks beat a retarded boy
    to death. The police report indicated
    he was hit by a car outside York, New York.
    His body was found in a gulley by the roadside.


2   And nothing,
    loose ends you tie up with your thoughts
    and force together.

    I take the wrong exit on an expressway in Buffalo,
    while the whole country turns over
    into another Saturday morning.

    There's no shade to draw, no light to turn off.
    The day splits open: tongues of steel flash
    in sunlight, broken stumps in a marshland.

    At a gas station
    they clean the windshield, wipe away the dirt.

3    On Route 80, near Tiffin, Iowa
     a car swerves on a blind hill
     and crashes into an oncoming pick-up truck.

     Two farmboys hear the moans the dead make,
     find the bodies still shaking
     in the throes of impact.

     One boy lifts a black man from behind
     the steering wheel, gets shit on his hands
     and swears.

     The police arrive.  The old woman in the pick-up
     gurgles, her face torn off, her husband dead
     in the seat beside her.

     The farmboys talk with the sheriff.
     The old woman doesn't cry.

## LETTER TO GWEN

Fall drags itself through its own month
an old man in the street
with the dogs barking.

In Cleveland I watch three cab drivers
toss pennies against the bus station wall,
the wind tucks itself behind my eyes,
I find myself moving away again.

My thoughts are those moments
I have kept tied up -
your hands parting white curtains,
the first light spreading its lace in the grass.

In Iowa it is raining.  I try and speak politely.
I go for long walks.

It's no use.
The old loneliness comes back,
that coat with the holes in the sleeves
I've worn all these years like armor.

Love, take the hand from your eyes,
let down your hair,
put out the light.

I drive back through the small towns,
the moon drifting sail-like above the trees,
the still fields before the snow.

All I can tell you are lies.
The days are numbered pages
pressed together neatly like your thighs.
The summer is behind us, a long hallway.

I have always loved you.

## FLIGHT INTO THE REAL

1    The dream is no dream.
Lifted to the glass
I fit my eye to the lens
and the distance is brought near:

I am seven and my grandfather
holds me up on the rail
and I can see the waterfalls
the white mist rising.

I thought then that becoming a man
was being big enough
to see without help.


2    Grandfather, you came to this country
lost wife and daughter in the first years,
saw the days fall to the children.

The railroad cars, the grapes you brought upstate
to sell to the men who still made wine;
the cigar smoke: talk I couldn't understand.

I remember the funeral,
my younger brother asking if we could stay
and watch the workmen at the grave.


3    Time does not stop. I've grown away
from your death into my own.
I always knew what I wanted to say:
in each thing there is deception.

Even now, another Spring presses
the clear, cold air.
*Speranza è verde,* you said.

The skin heals, the old scars fade to lines;
the mind in its own evolution -
a steady pressure to the rear
until the trigger is released.

## THE SOUND OF GUNS

### 1

The sparrow hawk drops to the cornfield
and in the same motion rises.
December's cold tightens around me,
a spider's web frozen white against the glass.

All day the sky is bleak with the coming snow,
the hours seem to pause like the bird
caught in an uplift of wind.
Out back the hay lies in rolls
the cows huddled together near the water troughs.

The highway runs past the brown fields
all the way west to Omaha, and just keeps going.
At the university in town
tight-lipped men tell me the war in Vietnam is over,
that my poems should deal with other things:
earth, fire, water, air.

### 2

A friend told me once
that ours was a generation of love;
and I know he meant that this was a generation
that took too much, that turned from one death
to another.

I don't know what it is that's kept me going.
At nineteen I stood at night and watched
an airfield mortared. A plane that was to take
me home, burning; men running out of the flames.

Seven winters have slipped away,
the war still follows me.
Never in anything have I found
a way to throw off the dead.

## THE FALL OF DANANG

Tonight the newspapers report
the air-lift evacuation of Danang has failed;
that South Vietnamese soldiers shot their way
through crowds of civilians
to board the last plane that landed.

Years have passed since Aubrey and I
got high together, watching the night sky
across the South China Sea.
Near Monkey Mountain the Viet-Cong are entrenched
hitting the airfield with artillery fire.

I think back to an evening in July
in that same city, when I waited for a plane
to get me out.
My friends watch television.

I pry open the window, listen to the noise
of a passing car on the wet road.
The news interrupts a commercial
with a special bulletin.  I watch the faces
of Vietnamese children: the same tired faces
that will always be there.

My friends leave to play poker:
nickel, dime, quarter, they say.
I smoke cigarettes, drink beer.
It's Saturday night, the end of March.

## THE WARRIORS
*[for Dave Kelly]*

*What does not change/ is the will to change—Charles Olson*

I    What survives
is the will to survive.

It was a street
a town he came back to
after a war,

a woman he was saying goodnight to
watching her shake his laughter
from her hair,

a spring when it rained for weeks
and in night fields
fireflies gathered.

What continues
is the dust.

A deserted station
a moth trapped in the light
outside a window.

II   He was walking through a wind -
     there was memory -

     a dirt road
     in the heat of afternoon
     watching the trucks approach
     the dust kicking up from the tires.

     And below on the ocean
     boats bringing their catch home,
     gulls following the wakes
     in hunger.

     In the mountains
     when it rains
     it seems to last forever.

III    He is not dead
       he is not sleeping
       he is walking on a dark street.

       The singer gives away her voice
       and begins again.
       The survivors are on the stairs
       with their teeth in their hands.

       The crows sit by the highway
       watching the cars
       and picking at the ground.

       The Indians believed the bringer of death
       had two faces

       each one moving so quickly
       in search of life

       that to one who saw the spirit
       it appeared faceless.

IV  Memory
    you begin with pain;

    a woman
    dressed as a woman,

    the night
    eating its way in.

    We come back to ourselves
    too often
    the ghosts in their grim circle.